Managing Poor Performance

handling staff capability issues

Maureen Cooper & Bev Curtis

Published by Network Educational Press Ltd.
PO Box 635
Stafford
ST16 1BF

First Published 2000
© Maureen Cooper and Bev Curtis 2000

ISBN 1 85539 062 0

Series Co-ordinator - Anat Arkin
Series Editor - Carol Etherington
Cover design by Neil Hawkins, Devine Design
Internal design and layout by Neil Gordon, Init Publishing
Illustrations by Barking Dog Art

Printed in Great Britain by
Redwood Books, Trowbridge, Wilts.

CONTENTS

INTRODUCTION

Staff are a school's most important - and most expensive - resource. The quality of teaching and learning, children's safety and well-being, and the ethos of the school all depend on the people who work in it. This may seem an obvious point, yet traditionally little attention has been paid in education to the skills required to manage staff and get the most out of them. Reports from OFSTED inspectors, for example, will sometimes say that the quality of teaching and learning in a school is unsatisfactory, but help with putting these weaknesses right is often hard to come by.

This practical handbook aims to provide schools with this much-needed help. It draws on the principles that apply to the management of performance in all areas of employment, but sets these firmly in the context of education. Case studies based on the authors' extensive experience of advising both primary and secondary schools on personnel issues are used throughout the book. Model documents, which readers may wish to adapt for use in their own schools, are also provided.

Like other titles in the Education Personnel Management series, *Managing Poor Performance,* is aimed primarily at senior managers in schools and members of the Governing Body's staffing committee. A summary of the role of governors in managing poor performers is included for the benefit of other governors, while a section examining the difficult issue of managing a headteacher's under-performance is intended to help chairs of governors to carry out their line management responsibilities in relation to headteachers.

Maureen Cooper and Bev Curtis

The following icons are used throughout the book to identify certain types of information:

Case Study

Legal

Checklist

Model Procedure

CHAPTER 1
PERFORMANCE MATTERS

Creating the right climate

Teachers in Britain have traditionally enjoyed a high degree of autonomy. As professionals, they were deemed to be competent, and what went on in the classroom rarely came under scrutiny.

This approach has now largely disappeared. OFSTED inspections have highlighted significant variations in teachers' and headteachers' performance, and led to a raft of government initiatives designed to raise standards of teaching and learning in all schools. High level pronouncements on the need to weed out poor teachers have also put the spotlight on the question of staff performance. While estimates of the number of incompetent teachers currently practising in our schools are the subject of heated debate, there is now a consensus that children's education suffers when teachers are not up to the job, and that schools need to manage the performance of their staff.

However, the culture in the education service has made it difficult to tackle performance issues. Whereas managers in other occupations usually view the management of people as a key part of their role, school managers have traditionally concentrated on managing the curriculum, rather than the people who deliver it or who carry out other functions in the school. In this culture, telling an employee that his or her work has fallen short of the mark is often seen as an adversarial action, which school managers are understandably often reluctant to take.

There is a pressing need to change this culture to one where schools deal with ineffective teachers as promptly and professionally as most already do with pupils who have fallen behind in their work. Few schools would dream of letting a pupil struggle for two or three terms, let alone two or three years, before taking steps to address the problem. The same, essentially supportive, approach needs to be taken with under-performing staff. If their needs were routinely addressed as soon as problems began to surface, discussions about performance would come to be seen as supportive, rather than adversarial, and schools would have a better chance of maintaining high standards of teaching and learning.

Defining 'capability'

Different LEA and school procedures use a variety of terms to discuss staff performance. They may talk about capability, incapability, competence, incompetence or performance management. In essence, these terms all refer to the same thing: the employee's ability to do the job; but it is important to be clear about the distinction between the school's Performance Management Policy, which is a form of appraisal, and capability procedures, which are solely designed to deal with under-performance.

In the case of a class or subject teacher, capability might be about classroom management and organisation, planning, marking or differentiation of work. For a head of department, it might additionally include departmental planning and resource management, while for a lunch-time supervisor it might be time management and pupil discipline. Capability can also refer to an employee's attitude. This is a tricky area as it is sometimes difficult to establish whether an inappropriate attitude reflects an employee's inability to do the job properly or an unwillingness to do it. If an employee is quite capable of doing the job but will not do it, then the issue is one of conduct, not of capability. Another handbook in this series, *Managing Challenging People*, gives advice on dealing with staff conduct.

This distinction is important, especially where concerns about an employee's conduct or capability ultimately lead to dismissal. If an employee brings a claim for unfair dismissal to an employment tribunal, the fairness of the dismissal will be tested in relation to the reasons given for it. So, for example, where a teacher with poor classroom management skills or patchy subject knowledge is sacked for misconduct, when in reality the issue is one of incompetence, a tribunal will almost certainly deem that dismissal unfair. In conduct cases, the punishment can fit the 'crime'. If misconduct is so serious that it amounts to gross misconduct, it can lead to an employee's summary dismissal. This is very rarely an option when capability is an issue, since employment law does not recognise such a thing as 'gross lack of capability'. When an employee's performance is less than satisfactory, managers are advised to go through every stage of their organisation's capability procedure. It is only if this fails to produce the necessary improvements that dismissal should be considered.

The only situation in which summary dismissal for incompetence might be fair is where an employee makes such a serious mistake that the employer cannot risk a repetition. The classic example is of an airline pilot whose incompetence endangers passengers' lives. Here, the risk of allowing the pilot time to improve would be too great and the employer would be justified in dismissing him or her straight away.

Similarly, if a teacher's mishandling of dangerous chemicals in the science lab were to result in the serious injury or death of a child, a school would perhaps be justified in moving straight to a dismissal hearing without first giving the individual any warnings. In such a case, however, the legal reason for the dismissal would probably be 'some other substantial reason', rather than capability; the substantial reason being that the safety of pupils was at risk. It should also be remembered that nobody, not even an airline pilot, becomes incompetent overnight, and therefore summary dismissal should only be considered in truly exceptional cases.

A capability checklist

- Capability is about a person's performance and ability to do the job.
- There is no such thing as 'gross lack of capability' or 'gross incompetence'.
- Other than in the most exceptional circumstances, employees cannot be dismissed for incompetence until every stage in the organisation's competence procedure has been followed in full.

A useful rule of thumb for distinguishing between issues of conduct and capability is to ask whether an employee can't or won't do something or act in a particular way.

Try applying this rule to the following situations to decide whether they raise issues of competence or capability.

Conduct or capability?

- A young history teacher in his second post has so much trouble maintaining discipline that colleagues complain about the noise coming from his classroom. He resigns after a year, complaining that his repeated requests for help with classroom management have been ignored.

- A school secretary does not always answer the telephone when it rings. When questioned about this, she says she is not able to drop what she is doing every time the phone rings. It turns out that she has never received any instructions or training in prioritising her work or how to deal with callers.

- An English teacher is not following her department's policy in setting and marking work for pupils. When challenged, she tells her head of department that she has her own methods of achieving results, which are more effective than "ploughing through piles of tedious marking".

The first of the above situations raises issues of competence, which could and should have been tackled by giving the employee concerned the training and support he so obviously needed. Indeed, if the history teacher had become ill as a result of being constantly stressed by the situation, or if he had resigned and then complained of constructive dismissal, the school could be required to show that it had acted reasonably and provided him with appropriate support. (It should be remembered that an employee now has the right to bring a claim for unfair dismissal to an employment tribunal after just one year in post, rather than two years, as in the past.)

The second example could be a case of either conduct or capability. If the secretary was simply being inflexible in her approach and attempting to dictate how the job should be done, that would be a matter of conduct. If, however, she was genuinely unable to handle more than one task at a time, that would clearly be a matter of capability.

By contrast, the English teacher in our third example is, by her own admission, deliberately failing to carry out an aspect of her job. Since she can, but won't, set and mark pupils' work, she should be dealt with under the school's conduct procedure.

Setting standards

Teachers and other employees in a school are entitled to know what is expected of them. Indeed, unless these expectations are clearly spelled out, it is impossible to judge whether a person's work is satisfactory or not. Therefore, schools need to consider performance standards for all staff within the context of their Performance Management policy.

For classroom teachers in both primary and secondary schools, the Teacher Training Agency's (TTA) national standards for qualified teacher status (QTS) provide a useful starting point. These cover knowledge and understanding, teaching, class management, planning, monitoring, assessment, recording, reporting and accountability. Intended to provide a baseline for assessing trainees seeking qualified teacher status, the standards can be adapted and developed to the circumstances of individual schools and the demands on both newly-qualified and more experienced teachers.

The TTA's standards for subject leaders and for special educational needs co-ordinators could be adapted in a similar way to set out what is expected of those in middle management roles. The experience gained from the Threshold Assessment process will also be very useful.

Where a teacher or manager falls short of expectations, the standards could also be used as a basis for targets for improvement. However, they should not be used to justify a crude checklist approach to the management of staff performance. As the Teacher Training Agency puts it in the introduction to the QTS standards, professionalism implies more than meeting a series of discrete standards. "It is necessary to consider the standards as a whole to appreciate the creativity, commitment, energy and enthusiasm which teaching demands."

The downward slide

When new members of staff are appointed to a school, there is obviously a presumption that they are capable of doing their jobs or they would not have been appointed in the first place. A period of induction is now mandatory for all newly-qualified teachers, and is also advisable for other newly-appointed members of a school's teaching and non-teaching staff. This should help new staff to settle in. However, headteachers are entitled to expect that, within a short space of time, a new employee will be performing at a satisfactory level.

Where the performance of recently appointed staff is well below that level, the school may need to review its staff selection and induction methods. With more established members of staff, however, managers need to ask when the decline in performance began. People do not perform at a satisfactory level one day and at a wholly unsatisfactory level the next. There is always a downward slide. If this has taken place over a period of time and line managers have not drawn the employee's attention to it, there may be two capability issues to address: that of the employee who is under-performing and that of the manager who has failed to tackle the situation.

Of course, none of us can say that our performance remains consistently good throughout our working lives. It varies from day to day, week to week and month to month, according to the challenges of the job, the state of our health and our personal circumstances. Usually, however, when our performance dips below the satisfactory line, it is only a short period before it climbs again - and perhaps we then perform above the line for periods of time. From a management point of view, the trick is to catch performance just as it begins to dip, and to put in measures to bring it back to a satisfactory level.

If the downward slide is allowed to continue, the hill the employee must climb gets steeper and steeper, and it becomes increasingly difficult to bring the individual's performance back to a satisfactory level. In addition, the further performance is allowed to slide, the more adversarial the situation is likely to become when it is eventually tackled. It is much easier for all concerned if under-performance is dealt with sooner rather than later as part of a wider process of supporting employees and contributing to their professional development.

From an employment law perspective, too, it is only fair to let an employee know that he or she is not doing the job properly. As soon as an employee's performance begins to slide below the level judged to be satisfactory, therefore, he or she should be warned about the situation. This explains why leaping straight to an assumption of 'gross incompetence' is inappropriate. If an employee had been summarily dismissed for incompetence without having received any previous warnings, an employment tribunal would be likely to find that dismissal unfair. It is vital that each stage of the school's competence procedure is followed.

Dealing with unsatisfactory performance

1 A lack of action

date of appointment

satisfactory performance

actual performance X ——————————————— 0

- Poor selection procedures;
- poor induction;
- poor management ... lead to poor results.

2 Waiting too long

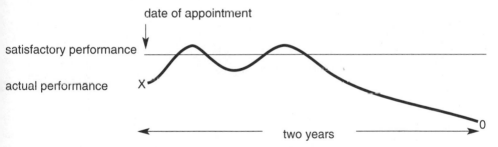

date of appointment

satisfactory performance

actual performance X

two years

The bigger the gap between desired and actual performance, the more management must bear the responsibility for not dealing with the problem promptly. If management does not start tackling the problem until 0 has been reached, the full capability process will still need to be followed:

- verbal warning;
- first written warning;
- final written warning;
- dismissal.

If the school tries to dismiss on the 'fast track' when 0 is reached, the dismissal could well be unfair because management has failed to formally warn the employee an earlier stage.

3 What should have happened

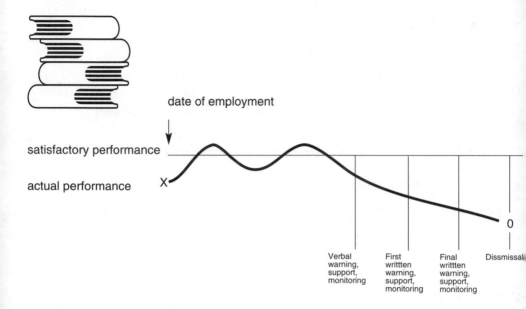

date of employment

satisfactory performance

actual performance X

0

| Verbal warning, support, monitoring | First writtten warning, support, monitoring | Final writtten warning, support, monitoring | Dissmissal |

Under-performing staff and the newly-appointed head

One of the most difficult situations that can face a newly-appointed headteacher is to find that several members of the school's teaching staff are under-performing. In the worst cases, poor management has allowed a culture of under-performance to develop, and the teachers concerned are oblivious to the problem because no-one has ever criticised their work.

In future, the Performance Management review process and the OFSTED cycle of inspections should mean that this situation arises less frequently than it used to. However, at present, OFSTED is still identifying cases where a culture of under-performance has been allowed to grow, and new headteachers are being drafted in to sort out schools which find themselves in special measures or have serious weaknesses.

Small rural primary schools are particularly at risk of developing a culture of under-performance. Often, this results from the unwitting collusion of parents and the local community. A teacher who has taught at the local primary school, perhaps for 20 years, is naturally an established and often highly respected member of the community, who may have taught the parents of his or her present pupils. When a new headteacher comes in and concludes that this teacher is not performing to a satisfactory level, then very often parents, the community and sometimes the school's own governors will view the headteacher as the problem, not the teacher. The following case study illustrates this point.

A new broom

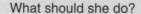

Ann Lister has recently been appointed headteacher of a small rural primary school with 126 pupils on roll. The school has three class teachers and one teacher employed for 60 per cent of the time to share Year 6 with Ann.

Ann soon discovers that Margaret Godwin, who takes Reception and Year 1, is not achieving acceptable standards with the pupils in her class. Mrs Godwin believes in waiting until children are ready to learn, and she has strong parental support for her approach. Many parents say that first and foremost they want their children to be happy at school.

The governors pride themselves on having a successful village school and they want the head to carry on where her predecessor, who retired after 25 years in the job, left off.

The school's last OFSTED report, four years ago, was satisfactory. A further inspection is now imminent, and Ann believes that standards of teaching and learning at Key Stage 1 are likely to be heavily criticised.

What should she do?

Firstly, she should attempt to educate the Governing Body. Difficult though it may be, Ann must get at least some governors to understand what can and should be expected in terms of achievement for each year group. The problem of a newly-appointed head being regarded as wrong, over-ambitious or "out of step with what we want for this school" can be partially - though not completely - solved by getting an external evaluation of the quality of teaching and learning in the school, for example from an LEA inspector or advisor.

Secondly, Ann should begin the process of managing Mrs Godwin's performance by:

- identifying what needs to be done and setting appropriate targets;
- giving Mrs Godwin a review date, by which time these targets should have been met;
- outlining what support and guidance will be available and ensuring that this is provided;
- explaining how progress will be monitored.

Identifying under-performance

Evidence that a teacher's performance is below par emerges in different ways. In some schools, nothing is done until parents begin to complain. In well managed schools, on the other hand, heads of department and other team leaders routinely use classroom observation to monitor the quality of teaching and learning in their departments or teams. Some schools have even started collecting feedback from pupils.

OFSTED inspections have brought the issue of staff performance out into the open since, each time an inspection takes place in a school, employees are left in no doubt as to how their performance has been assessed. However, inspectors' criticisms of a teacher's performance should be used only as a starting point for tackling the problem, and not as justification for moving straight to formal capability proceedings. No matter how evidence of poor performance emerges, a school should always use informal methods to help the individual reach the required standard, but only for half a term or so before resorting to the formal capability procedure.

The new performance management framework

Staff appraisal should, in theory, enable headteachers and team leaders to identify staff who are struggling. In the past, however, appraisals have been too infrequent and too much of a 'bolt-on' activity to provide a reliable method for identifying poor performance in many schools. There have even been cases where teachers who are clearly not up to the job still manage to get glowing appraisal reports!

The Government's performance management framework, in place from December 2000, will give schools a far more systematic methodology for dealing with performance issues than they have had in the past. By requiring schools to support and monitor all teachers' work, the framework will help managers to detect the first signs of under-performance.

Discussion of the new framework has focused largely on its controversial link with performance-related pay. However, a performance management system is potentially much more than a vehicle for delivering pay rises. While many of the systems used outside the education service are reward-driven, others are more concerned with identifying both high performers for possible promotion and poor performers who may need support or career counselling. These two approaches are not mutually exclusive and, ideally, the education service needs to adopt a model that combines the two.

Using the framework to manage under-performance

The statutory framework requires all schools to develop a written Performance Management policy. This should set out arrangements, linked to the school's development cycle, for agreeing, monitoring and reviewing objectives with every teacher.

A school's Governing Body needs to agree this policy and make sure that it operates effectively, but governors should not be involved in making judgements about individual teachers. It is the headteacher's responsibility to implement the school's Performance Management policy. This means making sure that objectives are agreed for all teachers, that their work is monitored and that regular reviews take place.

It is then up to heads of department or other team leaders to agree objectives with individual teachers. The starting point for this process is a clear job description which spells out the teacher's main responsibilities. The next step is to discuss his or her priorities in relation to pupils' needs, and to agree specific objectives for the coming year. The school improvement plan, any departmental development plans and information about pupils' prior attainment should inform this discussion.

Once objectives have been agreed, managers need to monitor the individual teacher's progress throughout the year. An annual review will then provide an opportunity to reflect on the teacher's performance, recognise achievements and identify areas for improvement and professional development. This review will also enable managers to detect any signs that the individual's performance has slipped.

Standard documentation and pro forma, such as those included in the DfEE's model performance management policy, should be used to guide line managers through the review process and ensure that all staff are treated in the same way.

Capability procedures and the performance management framework

Even though the performance management framework has an important role to play in identifying poor performance, it is entirely separate from a school's capability procedure. Once a school decides to use a formal capability procedure to deal with a struggling teacher, that procedure supersedes performance management arrangements.

Managing the performance of non-teaching staff

Although the performance management framework applies only to teachers, similar methods can be used to track the performance of non-teaching staff. Certainly, there is no reason why the work of school caretakers, office staff, lunch-time supervisors and other support staff should not come under the same kind of scrutiny as teachers. Agreeing objectives with members of the support staff, monitoring their work, reviewing it annually and supporting those who are not meeting their objectives will contribute to the smooth running of any school.

Empowering middle managers

In private industry, the job of spotting a downward trend in performance and beginning the process of reversing it usually falls to an employee's immediate line manager. So, in a bank or a supermarket, for example, it will be up to departmental supervisors in the first instance to manage the performance of sales staff, with the branch manager stepping in only if informal counselling and support fail to bring about an improvement.

In education, by contrast, we often disempower middle and senior managers other than the headteacher. Yet heads of department, deputy heads and other school managers have a crucial role to play in identifying poor performance and, at least in the early informal stages, of attempting to bring about improvements. After all, it is likely that they, rather than the headteacher, have day-to-day contact with members of their teams. There is also a risk that all but the most serious problems will be ignored if, on top of all their other duties, heads have sole responsibility for the process of dealing with poor staff performance.

There are three roles to play in this process. First, there is the role of judging whether an employee's work is less than satisfactory and deciding what action needs to be taken to improve it. The second role involves supporting, guiding and advising the employee, while the third role is to do with monitoring and evaluating progress.

In the initial stages, the individual's immediate line manager may play all three roles. The analogy here is with a teacher who would probably wear those three different hats automatically when dealing with a failing pupil. If a pupil has, for example, fallen behind with their reading, a teacher will usually discuss the problem with them, set some tasks designed to help them catch up and then keep a close eye on their progress. A head of department or other line manager needs to take a similar approach with staff whose work is causing concern.

CHAPTER 2
SUPPORTING POOR PERFORMERS

Beginning the process

We have already stressed the importance of identifying a dip in an individual's performance as soon as it occurs. The next task is to establish the probable cause of the problem. Managers will usually need to consider whether health issues or personal or domestic difficulties are contributory factors. Where this is the case, professional counselling or medical advice may help to reverse the decline in a teacher's performance.

It is, however, important to remember that the education of pupils is the reason why teachers are employed in schools. No matter how distressing a teacher's personal circumstances are, the headteacher's first responsibility is to the children. Therefore, concerns about the teacher's performance should never be swept under the carpet.

The situation is particularly difficult when, as often happens, an employee develops a stress-related illness after his or her performance has come under scrutiny. Again, this needs to be treated sympathetically, but managers should not allow sympathy to deter them from addressing performance issues once the employee has returned to work from sick leave. After a short period to allow the person to settle back into school, the headteacher or other manager handling the situation will need to tackle these still unresolved issues. This requires a face-to-face meeting, which, in the prevailing climate in schools, many headteachers and other school managers find extremely difficult to conduct. In fact, some find it so difficult that they avoid the task altogether and either take some of the struggling teacher's workload on to their own shoulders or allow children's education to suffer.

The trouble with Jim

Jim Collins, a science teacher in a large secondary school, has long had trouble maintaining discipline in his classes. For the last three years, Sarah Banks, the head of the science faculty, has been timetabled to teach next door to Jim so that she can intervene to restore order whenever pupils' behaviour gets out of hand. Sometimes, Sarah also removes difficult pupils from Jim's classes and supervises them herself. Recently, this has been happening more and more frequently, and Sarah is finding that she is spending several hours a week supporting Jim and offering him guidance and suggestions.

Sarah is effectively now doing part of Jim's job for him. What is more, she has been doing this for far too long, and in all probability Jim has come to rely on it, and indeed to see it as part of his entitlement. If this situation is allowed to continue, before long there will be two performance problems because Sarah will not be able to carry out all her own responsibilities as head of faculty on top of doing part of Jim's job for him. Jim's growing dependence on Sarah's help also has financial implications for the school, as when any manager 'over-supports' a team member.

With Jim's pupils achieving significantly poorer SATs and examination results than those taught in parallel classes, and both parents and pupils complaining, John Beckett, the school's headteacher, has finally decided that something must be done. Since Jim has never had an oral warning, even though his colleagues have known about his problems for years, the head needs to begin at the beginning of the school's capability procedure.

The head asks Sarah to produce a short report of her concerns and the support and guidance she has already given Jim. He then discusses his intended course of action with her and hears that Sarah is worried about the role she might be asked to play. She explains that the members of her faculty have always worked together as a team and she does not want to destroy their trust in her.

The head takes the view that Sarah has formed an inappropriate 'colleague-as-friend' relationship with Jim, and that there is not sufficient distance between them for her to take on a monitoring role in relation to his performance.

He therefore decides that the monitoring of Jim's performance and progress towards the set targets should be carried out by someone from outside the school. He also notes that there is an urgent need for Sarah to have in-service training in performance management issues, a key part of any team leader's job.

Following his discussion with Sarah, John Beckett sets out the following course of action.

Intended course of action

1. Discuss concerns with Jim.
2. Set targets for improvement.
3. Arrange for head of faculty to provide support and guidance.
4. Arrange for external science adviser to monitor performance.
5. Set review date.

The head then arranges a meeting with Jim to discuss the situation.

In arranging this meeting, the head has done the following:

- He has reached a view that the concerns about Jim's performance are serious and that, since Jim has already received support over a period of time, the seriousness of the situation needs to be spelled out to him. In other words, the time has come to give Jim an oral warning or, at the very least, 'strong advice'.

- He has re-read the school's capability procedure and noted that, since an oral warning is not part of the formal procedure, Jim is not entitled to be accompanied by a union official or anyone else at the meeting. Nevertheless, he decides that he will make an exception to the usual practice and let the science teacher bring someone along to support him. He does this in the hope that, 'behind the scenes', Jim's representative will point out that the head's expectations are quite reasonable.

- He has also decided to have an external adviser present at the meeting.

The headteacher writes Jim the following letter.

3 March 2000

Dear Jim,

I would like to meet you on Thursday 10 March at 2.00 p.m. in my office to discuss the following concerns that I have regarding your performance as a teacher:

1   management of student behaviour;
2   planning and, in particular, differentiating the work you set for pupils;
3   delivery of lessons, in particular the challenge, pace and variety of your teaching.

This meeting will be a professional discussion and not part of the school's formal capability procedure. However, since the meeting may result in an oral warning, you may, exceptionally, be accompanied by a trade union representative or a colleague if you wish. Mrs Pam Brown, the school's personnel adviser, and Ms Sarah Banks, your head of faculty, will also be present.

Yours sincerely,

John Beckett, Headteacher

Conducting a professional discussion

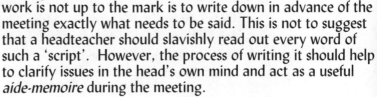

One way of approaching the difficult task of telling an employee that his or work is not up to the mark is to write down in advance of the meeting exactly what needs to be said. This is not to suggest that a headteacher should slavishly read out every word of such a 'script'. However, the process of writing it should help to clarify issues in the head's own mind and act as a useful *aide-memoire* during the meeting.

The script needs to avoid generalities and should set out the nature of the problem in very specific terms. For example, it may be useful to compare assessment data or examination results achieved by the teacher's pupils with those of pupils taught by other members of staff. It should also set out a series of manageable targets and describe the support measures that will be put in place to help the employee achieve these targets by a given review date.

This date is crucial because, if matters are left open-ended, the chances are that the situation will be left to drift.

The script can then be turned into a memorandum of the meeting, and a copy given to the employee so that there is no doubt on either side as to what the problems are and how they are going to be addressed. The memorandum should also include a summary of comments the employee has made during the meeting.

Script for professional discussion with Jim Collins

In the example of our under-performing science teacher, Jim Collins, his headteacher might prepare the following script in advance of their professional discussion.

1. Introductions

It is important for the head to establish that this is his meeting. If Jim decides to bring someone with him, that person should play a supporting role and not be allowed to dictate the conduct of the meeting.

Introduce those present to each other.

2. Set the Agenda

By briefly running through what will be discussed, the headteacher will be able to make the structure of the meeting clear and purposeful. Jim will also know what to expect and, while he may wish to 'clarify' certain points, he will only be able to object if something that the head says is factually wrong. These objections can be noted, but the head should keep control of the meeting and stick to what he has planned to say.

2.1 This meeting is a professional discussion and not part of the school's formal capability procedure.

2.2 The purpose of the meeting is to set out the areas of concern, provide an opportunity for Jim Collins to respond and to set out:
a) the targets to be met;
b) the programme of support and monitoring that will be put in place;
c) an agreed date when the situation will be reviewed.

The head should refer to Jim's strengths as well as his weaknesses and be as specific as possible about his shortcomings. The head should also give an indication of the evidence that has been used to identify each area of concern. This evidence does not have to be of the standard expected in a court of law, but it does need to provide a factual basis for a reasoned professional judgement. As each concern is outlined, Jim should be given an opportunity to respond. Very often, teachers who have problems with student behaviour will say that many of their colleagues have similar problems with those students. While this may be true, it should not deflect head from his planned course of action in relation to Jim's particular problems.

3. Outline the concerns

3.1 Management of pupil behaviour
The problem:
- A significant number of pupils, especially in Years 9 and 10, are often not 'on task' and consequently disrupt other pupils' learning.
- Jim's strategies for dealing with off-task behaviour are confrontational and unsuccessful.

Evidence of the problem:
- the high number of referrals to the head of faculty for behaviour management support;
- complaints from parents and pupils.

3.2. Differentiation of work set for pupils
The problem:
- The work Jim sets does not reflect pupils' different levels of ability and understanding. In particular, it does not challenge more able students.

Evidence of the problem:
- the head of faculty's observations on lesson planning;
- complaints from pupils and parents.

3.3 Delivery of lessons, in particular challenge, pace and variety of methodology
The problem:
- Jim makes excessive uses of 'chalk and talk' and OHPs. His pace is usually quite slow and his voice monotonous.

Evidence of the problem:
- the head of faculty's observations of his teaching;
- complaints from parents and pupils.

The head of faculty has been meeting Jim regularly over a long period of time to give him support and guidance. Jim has also been timetabled to teach next to her classroom so that she can intervene when difficulties arise - something she has been doing more and more often of late.

4. Describe the support Jim has already received.

5. Set Jim the following targets:

5.1 To achieve satisfactory levels of pupil co-operation and on-task behaviour.

5.2 To plan lessons which provide a variety of tasks and which challenge all pupils, in particular the more able.

5.3 To deliver lessons using a variety of whole-class, group and individual teaching strategies.

The head will have thought through the various possibilities in advance of the meeting.

6. Programme of support and guidance:

6.1 Weekly meetings with head of faculty to discuss progress and seek guidance.

6.2 Opportunity to observe an Advanced Skills Teacher in another school.

6.3. Attendance at a one-day behaviour management course.

7. Monitoring and evaluation:

7.1 The LEA's science adviser will observe Jim's lessons in around three weeks' time and then again after a further three weeks.

8. Review date and warning:

The situation will be reviewed after eight weeks. If, by that time, Jim has not made sufficient progress towards achieving the targets, the matter will be considered formally under the school's capability procedure.

After the meeting, the head sends Jim the following memorandum.

Memorandum of the meeting

From: John Beckett, headteacher
To: Jim Collins, science teacher
cc: Pam Brown, personnel adviser
Sarah Banks, head of science faculty

Note of professional discussion held on 10 March 2000

Present: Mr John Beckett, headteacher
Mr Jim Collins, science teacher
Mr Brian Searle, trade union official (supporting Mr Collins)
Ms Sarah Banks, head of science faculty
Mrs Pam Brown, personnel adviser

As indicated to you in my letter of 4 March 2000, the purpose of the meeting was to discuss concerns relating to your performance as a science teacher. These related to:

- management of student behaviour;
- planning and, in particular, differentiating the work you set for pupils;
- delivery of lessons, in particular the challenge, pace and variety of your teaching.

We discussed the extensive support that you have received from Sarah Banks and I indicated to you that this level of support could not continue indefinitely. You raised the point that the students you find challenging also present difficulties for other staff. I accept that this is the case but nevertheless take the view that your skills in managing student behaviour are insufficiently developed. We have agreed the following targets, which will be reviewed on 2 May 2000.

1. You will achieve satisfactory levels of pupil co-operation and on-task behaviour. (By 'satisfactory', I mean that Sarah will no longer have to intervene in your lessons.)
2. You will plan lessons that provide a variety of tasks and challenge all pupils, in particular for the more able.
3. You will deliver lessons using a variety of whole-class, group and individual teaching strategies.

Between now and the review date, Sarah will continue to provide you with a high level of support by meeting with you once a week to discuss your progress and give you advice. In addition, arrangements will be made for you to observe an Advanced Skills Teacher of science at High Hill School and you will be registered for the behaviour management training course which the LEA is holding on 20 April 2000.

Your progress will be monitored by Andrew Duncan, the LEA's science adviser, who will observe your lessons on two separate occasions during the review period.

I indicated to you that everything that is reasonably possible will be done to help you to improve your performance in the areas outlined above. I also warned you that, if your work has not shown improvement in these areas by the review date, I shall consider the matter formally under the school's capability procedure. I hope that this will not be necessary. As I told you at our meeting, I have always been impressed by your enthusiasm for your subject, and believe that you are capable of improving your performance in the classroom.

John Beckett, Headteacher

Improving classroom management, teaching and planning

The most common performance problems in schools concern classroom management, teaching and planning. Teachers with problems in these areas can be supported in a variety of ways, including the following.

'Sitting next to Nelly'

One of the most effective ways of helping a teacher maintain discipline in class, structure a lesson or improve any other aspect of performance is to demonstrate how things should be done. This means releasing the teacher to work alongside a more expert colleague or to observe that colleague's own teaching. The under-performing teacher may find this support less threatening if it comes from an experienced and successful teacher, possibly an Advanced Skills Teacher in another school. Where this is not practicable, the teacher should be given the opportunity to observe good practice in his or her own school. This will need to be over a sustained period: on at least two or three occasions over the time set for the teacher to reach agreed targets. A one-off observation session is far less likely to bring about a change in the individual's behaviour.

Tutorial support

One-to-one 'tutorials' with an experienced colleague or an external adviser are another way of supporting struggling teachers. This form of support is most useful when it includes observation of the teacher's lessons, with immediate feedback from the 'tutor'. However, the teacher will need to feel confident that this observation and feedback are truly supportive and do not form part of the monitoring and evaluation process.

Training

External or in-house training also has a role to play in supporting under-performing teachers. Ideally, however, training should be used in conjunction with work-based support. This will help to ensure that the 'high' that people often experience on courses leads to sustained improvement back at the chalkface.

Whatever method of support is used, it is important to build in time for discussion. There is little point in observing a teacher's performance if the information that comes out of the process is not shared with the person concerned.

Improving the performance of managers

People have traditionally been promoted to senior posts in schools as a result of their strengths as teachers, and there has been little in the way of management development to prepare them for these posts. While this may now be changing, there are still many heads of department or deputy heads who find themselves out of their depth as far as their management responsibilities are concerned.

Dealing with an ineffective head of department or deputy head is much like dealing with any other member of staff whose performance is not up to the mark. First of all, clear performance standards are needed to ensure that people in these roles understand exactly what is expected of them. The Teacher Training Agency's standards for subject leaders and special educational needs co-ordinator may be helpful in setting out these expectations.

If a manager's performance begins to slide, his or her own line manager will need to use target-setting and informal counselling and support to achieve improvement. As with class teachers, support and guidance can come either from an external source or a senior colleague from within the school. As well as observing the way the person in question runs meetings or approaches departmental planning, the expert may work alongside the manager for a time. Coupled with immediate feedback, these methods of support will often lead to improvements. The growing number of training programmes targeted at subject leaders and other school managers may also help.

Improving the performance of non-teaching staff

Again, the principles for dealing with non-teaching staff whose performance gives cause for concern are the same as for dealing with teachers. School secretaries, caretakers, lunch-time supervisors and classroom assistants need to know what is expected of them and, when they fall short of expectations, to know the precise nature of their shortcomings. They should then be set targets for improvement and given support to enable them to reach those targets. Their progress should be monitored and reviewed after a reasonable period of time.

Setting a time limit for counselling and support

Very often, under-performing staff in schools will receive informal counselling and support for an extended period of time, sometimes even for years. Eventually, frustration will lead some headteachers to attempt to resolve the problem quickly by removing the employee from the school. As we have indicated earlier, however, it is likely to be unlawful to move straight to dismissal in capability cases. Employers who fail to go through all the stages of their organisation's capability procedures may end up having to justify their actions to an employment tribunal, which can award damages of up to £50,000 to employees who have been unfairly dismissed.

The best way to resolve staff performance problems within a reasonable time-frame is to set clear limits for how long employees can expect to receive counselling and support. Between half a term and a term should give most people ample time to improve. If they do not, it will be time to adopt the more formal approach that we consider in the next chapter.

'What if...' procedures for managing under-performance

Things do not always go according to plan when it comes to managing under-performance. Here are some suggested solutions to problems that may occur:

- If the teacher refuses to attend a professional discussion unless a union representative is present, point out that, since this meeting does not form part of the school's formal capability procedure, there is no entitlement to representation. However, it is unwise to be drawn into a confrontation over what is, essentially, a side issue. It may even turn out turn out to be helpful to have a representative present, as behind the scenes this person may tell the teacher that management's concerns are not unreasonable. Do not, however, allow the union to dictate to you what should happen.

- If the teacher goes off sick when the discussion is due to take place, reschedule the meeting. However, if the teacher repeatedly uses sickness absence as a means of avoiding the problem, consider dealing with this as a misconduct issue.

- If the teacher claims that his or her line manager is not offering appropriate support, investigate the truth of this allegation. There may be a need to address issues concerning the manager's own competence.

- If the teacher says that everyone has problems with a particular group of pupils, point out that, while this may be true, the teacher's own problems still need to be addressed. If a teacher refuses to acknowledge that there is a problem, produce evidence to support your assessment of the situation. This could include complaints from pupils or parents, extracts from OFSTED reports and notes of your own classroom observations.

CHAPTER 3
FORMAL CAPABILITY PROCEDURES

The legal context

Since capability procedures vary from school to school, it is important that governors, headteachers and other managers are familiar with the workings of their own school's procedure. They also need to have some understanding of the legal implications of setting out on a road that may lead to an employee's dismissal.

 Employment law recognises just five fair reasons for dismissal. These are conduct, capability, statutory enactment, redundancy and some other substantial reason. 'Statutory enactment' covers those situations where an employer cannot legally continue to employ someone, for example because he or she is an overseas national without a valid UK work permit. 'Some other substantial reason' usually applies only to senior posts and might include, for example, a situation where the Governing Body of a school has lost all confidence in the headteacher or where continuing to employ an individual could put children's safety at risk.

It is important to be very clear about the reasons for dismissing an employee since, as we have already mentioned, an employment tribunal will judge the fairness of a dismissal in relation to the reasons given for it. If an employee should make a claim for unfair dismissal, the tribunal will also ask whether the process leading up to that dismissal has been fair. In this context, fairness means giving the employee a chance to improve, providing appropriate guidance and support and, when this fails to achieve results, following every stage of the school's capability procedure.

Education law, in particular Schedules 16 and 17 of the School Standards and Framework Act 1998, sets out the mechanisms for dismissing school employees either for incapability or one of the four other grounds. A committee consisting of at least three members of the school's Governing Body must consider the complaint and give the employee a chance to put his or her case either directly or though a representative. The Act also gives an employee the right to appeal against dismissal to an appeals committee of the Governing Body. Both legislation and the principles of natural justice demand that the appeals committee should be made up of governors who have had no involvement in the original decision to dismiss and are therefore impartial.

The appeals process itself can take one of two forms. Under some school or LEA procedures, the appeals committee will consider only new evidence or technical arguments as to why the original dismissal decision should be overturned. In other procedures, the appeal is effectively a re-hearing of the entire case. A re-hearing is usually worth the time and effort involved because case law has established that a procedural error in an original hearing can be rectified at the appeals stage. With improperly constituted panels and other procedural errors being the most common reason for employment tribunals finding in favour of employees in unfair dismissal cases, schools must make strenuous efforts to get the procedures right.

It is also worth noting that the dismissal of an employee in a maintained school does not come into force until the appeals process has been exhausted. Even at that point, an employee in a community or voluntary controlled school is not technically sacked until the local education authority has issued a notice of dismissal. (In foundation and aided schools, the notice of dismissal is issued by the Governing Body.) If a case reaches an employment tribunal, the date of dismissal will often be considered, and if a teacher's pay has been stopped before the employer has issued a dismissal notice, the dismissal may be deemed unfair.

Staff management and the law

The impact of employment and education law on the management of staff in schools is discussed in more detail in another handbook in the Education Personnel Management series, *Managing Challenging People*. Some of the key points that school managers need to consider are summarised below.

A checklist of key points to consider

- Employees can now bring claims for unfair dismissal after just one year in post.

- Employment law recognises just five fair reasons for dismissal, one of which is capability. A dismissal must be fair in relation to the reason(s) given for it. Governing Bodies of all maintained schools with delegated budgets have full responsibility for managing and disciplining staff, though legally the LEA is the employer in community and voluntary controlled schools.

- In community and voluntary controlled schools, the LEA has the right to give advice throughout any disciplinary or capability procedures relating to teaching staff.

- Foundation and aided schools may give the LEA advisory rights in relation to staff discipline and dismissal.

- Governors are not obliged to follow the LEA's advice but, if they wilfully ignore sound advice and consequently lose an unfair dismissal case, any compensation awarded for unfair dismissal may have to come out of the school's delegated budget.

- Governors in all types of schools may delegate responsibility for staff discipline up to the level of final written warning to the headteacher. In capability cases, they are strongly advised to do so.

Oral warnings

Where a reasonable period of informal counselling and support fails to improve performance, the employee should receive an oral warning. Sometimes called a verbal warning, this is not normally part of a school's formal capability procedure but is intended to serve as a managerial warning shot. Some procedures do, however, make it part of the formal procedure and give employees a right to appeal against an oral warning to the appeals committee of the school's Governing Body. In most cases, however, there is no right of appeal as this is thought to be at odds with the idea of firing a warning shot across the employee's bows.

In many schools, responsibility for disciplinary sanctions against staff up to the level of a final written warning rests solely with the headteacher. This means that oral warnings are usually given by the head. In large secondary schools, however, heads and governors need to consider if this is the best way to handle disciplinary matters. If the term 'middle management' is to have any meaning then, as we have already argued, heads of department and other team leaders ought to have full responsibility for managing their staff. In many organisations outside the education service, that includes responsibility for first-line disciplinary action, and there is no reason why schools should be any different.

After issuing an oral warning, the head or other line manager again needs to put in place measures to help the employee to reach clearly defined targets within a reasonable period of time.

The first written warning

The period between an oral warning and a first written warning can be varied according to the circumstances of each case, but it has to be reasonable. It must also take account of the so-called 'fast-track' outline capability procedure produced in 1997 by the National Employers' Organisation for School Teachers, in consultation with the teachers' unions. This procedure is not, in fact, as fast-track as some of its critics have maintained. Introduced because of concerns that many LEA procedures were overly-cumbersome and that schools were taking too long to resolve capability issues, the outline procedure indicates that under-performing staff should be given no more than two terms from the date of entry into the formal procedure to improve. It also provides that, in extreme cases, the period given for improvement should be no more than four weeks, though there is little evidence that schools are making much use of this aspect of the procedure.

The outline procedure does not cover capability due to ill-health, though the principles that apply in such instances are largely the same. (We consider the whole area of staff health and school effectiveness in another handbook in the Education Personnel Management series, *The Well Teacher*.)

The National Employers' outline procedure refers only to teachers, but some local procedures also apply it to non-teaching staff. Certainly, it makes sense for employers to use the same procedure with all staff, though the four-week 'fast-track' element may be less appropriate in relation to caretakers and lunch-time supervisors than teachers.

If, at the end of the period specified in the oral warning, the headteacher or head of department considers that the employee's performance has still not improved, or not improved sufficiently, a meeting with them should be arranged.

The headteacher will need to write to the employee in advance informing him or her of:

- the date, time and place of the meeting;
- the nature of the concerns about the employee's capability;
- the right to come to the meeting accompanied by a trade union representative or other person;
- any documents that will be used as evidence, with copies enclosed;
- the names of any witnesses who will be called.

A copy of this letter should be sent to whoever the employee has chosen as a representative.

The aim of the meeting is to improve performance, not to punish. It should certainly not be used to bully or harangue a struggling employee but should be conducted as calmly, objectively and fairly as possible. However, a headteacher cannot be expected to come to the meeting with a completely open mind, since the meeting would not have been called in the first place unless there were genuine concerns about the employee's performance.

The following checklist is intended to help ensure that employees are given a fair hearing and that managers come to a sound decision based on the facts of the case.

Considering a first written warning

Managers should consider the following questions:

- Has the employee been set clear performance standards?
- Has the employee received adequate training and guidance?
- What help and support has the employee received so far? Was this adequate?
- Are domestic or medical factors affecting his or her performance? If so, has appropriate counselling or medical help been offered?
- In the case of a teacher, what effect is his or her poor performance having on pupils' achievement?
- What was the employee's previous record and length of service?

If, following the meeting, the headteacher decides on the basis of the facts that complaints about the employee's capability are justified, the employee should be given a first written warning. The warning letter (or an appendix to the letter) should make clear:

- what aspects of the employee's performance are causing concern;
- what targets the employee will be expected to reach within a specified time;
- what support will be provided to help the employee reach these targets;
- how the employee's progress will be monitored and assessed;
- who will be carrying out this assessment;
- how long the assessment will last.

The warning letter should also explain that failure to meet the required standards may lead to a final written warning, but that if the employee's performance improves before or by the end of the assessment period, the written warning will be disregarded.

A first written warning is a formal sanction and the school's procedures will almost certainly provide for a right to appeal against it to the appeals committee of the Governing Body.

In most schools, a first written warning is issued by the headteacher, but there are some procedures where this is handled by a panel of governors. In the latter case, it is very important that:

- the panel empowered to dispense warnings (and to dismiss staff) is completely separate and has a different membership from the appeals panel;
- governors have some understanding of the performance issues about which they are being asked to make a judgement.

The final written warning

Towards the end of the assessment period specified in the first written warning, the headteacher will be forming a view about whether or not performance has reached a satisfactory level. This view should be based on the evidence provided by the person carrying out the monitoring and evaluation role. If there is no progress, or insufficient progress, it will be necessary to call the employee to a further meeting.

If this meeting results in a final written warning, again the letter will need to set out which aspects of the employee's performance will be assessed and the time-frame for that assessment. It will also have to explain that failure to meet the required standards will lead to a recommendation that the governors' staff dismissal committee should dismiss the employee. There is a right of appeal against a final written warning to the appeals committee of the Governing Body.

Disciplinary procedures sometimes provide for a second written warning, but this additional stage makes the whole process of dealing with capability far longer and more complicated than it needs to be, and is, in fact, one of the reasons why the Secretary of State for Education and Employment decided to require Governing Bodies to adopt the National Employers' Organisation's outline procedure.

As an alternative to referring the matter to the dismissal committee, the head and governors could consider offering the employee in question different duties or even a completely different post at a lower salary. This may be the best way forward in a situation where the school's procedures include this option and where a previously successful classroom teacher began to under-perform only after being promoted to a middle-management role. However, the individual would have to agree to take on the new role and the discussions surrounding it would need to be conducted very carefully because excessive pressure to agree to a demotion might result in a claim for constructive dismissal.

Dismissal

The final stage in any capability procedure is dismissal by a committee of governors, with, of course, a right of appeal to the appeals committee of the Governing Body.

Normally, the clerk to the governors will write a letter requiring the employee to attend a hearing before the governors' staff dismissal committee. This letter should contain the same details as the letter sent in relation to the earlier meetings or hearings. It is very important that the employee is warned that the hearing may result in his or her dismissal on the grounds of incapability. A failure to make it absolutely clear that the hearing could lead to dismissal leaves the door open for the employee to argue that he or she did not realise how serious the situation was. It may be appropriate for an employee to be suspended on full pay pending the outcome of the hearing.

The governors may decide not to dismiss but to issue a further written warning for a specified period. If the governors do decide to dismiss, written confirmation of the decision and the reasons for it needs to be sent to the employee, his or her representative and, in the case of community and voluntary controlled schools, to the LEA. The letter to the employee should make it clear that there is a right of appeal against the decision and should indicate how and by what date an appeal can be made. The conduct of the disciplinary hearing itself is considered in the next chapter.

Compromise agreements

Dismissal is always a difficult process for all concerned. Where an employee has received all the help and support the school can reasonably be expected to provide, and it is clear that no real improvement has occurred or is likely to occur, a compromise agreement offers an alternative to dismissal.

A compromise agreement offers the employer a legal means of ending a person's employment without the risk of the employee claiming unfair dismissal. There is a sum of money attached to the deal, which is up to the employee and his or her representative to negotiate, but the equivalent of between one and three terms' salary is not unusual.

A checklist for possible compromise agreement

No-one should ever be pressed into signing a compromise agreement. The employee must take independent legal advice from a qualified solicitor before acceding to the terms of the agreement. In schools, these terms usually include the following.

- The employee agrees to leave his or her post in return for specified compensation for loss of office. This sum is free of income tax and other deductions.
- In consideration of this payment, the employee agrees not to bring any claim against the Governing Body for unfair dismissal, sex, race or disability discrimination or any other matter connected to his or her employment at the school.
- The headteacher undertakes to provide any possible or future employer with an agreed reference. A copy of this reference may be attached to the agreement. Any oral references given subsequently need to be consistent with the written reference.
- The employer agrees to return any items belonging to the school, especially keys.
- All parties to the agreement undertake not to make any disparaging statements about each other and to keep the terms of the agreement strictly confidential.

Roles and responsibilities in managing capability procedures

In the early stages of tackling a staff capability issue, it is probably best for the headteacher or the employee's line manager to deal with all aspects of the matter. Once formal capability proceedings have begun, however, it is preferable for different people to play the judging, supporting and monitoring roles that we discussed in Chapter 1. This separation of the three roles is especially important in a small school where staff are in close day-to-day contact with each other and it may be awkward for the same person to provide a teacher with a supportive shoulder to cry on one day and to assess that person's performance the next.

Where counselling and support have failed to bring the employee up to the required standard, it is appropriate for the headteacher to take on the judgmental role and decide whether to issue an oral warning. Someone else could then play the non-critical and supportive role of confidant. It is important that the person playing this role should be truly supportive, since the aim is to help a struggling employee improve performance, rather than to find reasons to get rid of that person.

There are no rules about who can provide support. It may be the individual's line manager, a deputy or other senior teacher or an external adviser. Whoever plays the supportive role will, of course, have to enlist the employee's co-operation. If the employee rejects the offer of support and the school has done everything it reasonably can to help to raise that person's performance, the governors will be deemed to have carried out their responsibility in this respect if the matter ends up before an employment tribunal.

The third role in managing capability involves monitoring and evaluating whether the employee has reached his or her targets. This role is crucial because it is evidence from the monitoring process that will enable the head to decide what to do next. It is important, therefore, that the person responsible for monitoring and evaluating performance looks at the employee's performance fairly early on during the review period and gives the person some immediate feedback. A further evaluation later on will establish what progress, if any, has been made.

In any formal hearing to consider capability, the person who has monitored and evaluated performance will be the main witness as to whether or not the agreed targets have been reached. Again, there are no hard and fast rules about who might carry out this role, but clearly it has to be someone with sufficient credibility and experience - probably a deputy head or other senior member of staff. Sometimes, the school's procedures will specify who will normally take on this role.

Where there is a significant gap between actual and desired performance, it may be helpful to give the monitoring and evaluating role to an outsider such as an LEA inspector. The involvement of someone from outside the school will provide an element of objectivity and lessen the likelihood of the under-performing employee complaining of victimisation. Employees in this situation will sometimes say that their competence has been called into question only because of a personality clash with their headteacher or line manager. Managers should examine their own conduct and motivation to make sure this is not the case.

Unfortunately, there are some managers who do resort to bullying and harassing staff, usually because they themselves are not up to the job. An LEA inspector or other person from outside the school may find it easier to challenge such inappropriate management behaviour than one of the head's own subordinates.

Occasionally, an employee whose effectiveness has been called into question will attempt to start a grievance procedure against the headteacher. Whether or not the grievance is justified, no member of staff should ever be allowed to by-pass capability proceedings in this way. Any complaint the employee wishes to make against the head or other manager should be raised in the course of these proceedings.

CHAPTER 4
DISSMISSAL
HEARINGS

Arranging a dismissal hearing

Dismissal hearings are not an everyday occurrence in any school. So, before a hearing is held, the governors who make up the staff dismissal committee should be briefed on the procedure that will be followed. This task will normally be handled by a personnel adviser or education officer, who will also play an important part in the hearing itself.

The letter summoning a member of staff to a disciplinary hearing must comply with the requirements laid down in the school's formal disciplinary procedure. If this includes a requirement to provide documentary evidence in advance of the hearing, for example, then failure to comply may give the employee the right to seek a postponement.

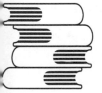

Letter summoning an employee to a hearing before the governors' staff dismissal committee

Dear ....,

I request your attendance at a hearing before the staff dismissal committee of the school's Governing Body. This will held on [date] at [place] at [time].

At the hearing, I shall recommend that you are dismissed from your post on the grounds of your lack of capability as a teacher.

You have the right to be accompanied or represented at the hearing by a representative of a trade union or some other person of your choice.

The following documents will be produced by the school in evidence:

-
-
-

In addition, the following witnesses will be called:

-
-
-

I shall be accompanied at the hearing by ..., who will act as my adviser.

Would you please let me know as soon as possible whether or not you will be represented and, if so, the name and position of your representative.

You or your representative have the right to produce documentary evidence and to call witnesses on your behalf. Please let me have (at least four days before the hearing) the names of any witnesses you propose to call and copies of any documents you intend to produce.

If you do not attend the hearing without good cause, the members of the dismissal committee may decide to proceed in your absence. A copy of this letter is enclosed for your representative.

Yours sincerely,

....
Headteacher

Conducting a dismissal hearing

There are different ways of conducting dismissal hearings. In some cases, the headteacher will present the school's case, while in others it will be presented by an LEA personnel officer or other professional adviser. Since heads are unlikely to undertake this task on a regular basis, our advice is that the school's case should be presented by someone with experience of handling such matters. Union officials representing employees usually have considerable experience of dismissal hearings, and a headteacher's lack of experience could easily undermine the school's case. It is also difficult for a headteacher to both present the case effectively and act as a witness.

When the three or more governors making up the staff dismissal committee have elected a chair and are ready to begin, the two 'sides' should be invited in to the meeting. The chair of the committee should introduce everyone and explain why the hearing is being held and how it will be conducted. He or she should then invite the school's representative to present the case for dismissal. This will normally consist of an opening statement, followed by the calling of witnesses in support of the school's case.

This case needs to be presented as clearly and succinctly as possible. A dismissal hearing is the culmination of a detailed process, and the person representing the school needs to help governors to focus on the main issues, without becoming immersed in minutiae. The presentation should therefore take the form of a chronological account of the key events leading up to the hearing.

To illustrate these points, we return to Jim Collins, the struggling science teacher we have met in earlier chapters and who, despite a considerable amount of support and two formal warnings, has still not improved sufficiently.

The school's case

After the introductions:

Chair: You will all be aware that we are here today to consider the dismissal of Jim Collins on the grounds of his alleged inability to carry out his responsibilities as a teacher to the required standard. I'd like to begin by inviting the school's personnel adviser, Mrs Pam Brown, to present the case for dismissal.

PB: Thank you, madam chairman. My purpose this morning is to demonstrate to the committee, through the witnesses I shall be calling and the written evidence I shall be presenting, that the school's capability procedure has been fully followed in every detail and that Jim Collins has been given every opportunity to improve his performance. Despite the considerable support he has received and the warnings he has been given at appropriate stages in the procedure, there has, regrettably, been little or no evidence of improvement. In the circumstances, it is both fair and reasonable to dismiss Mr Collins...

I'd now like to call Mr John Beckett, who as the school's headteacher, will be our main witness. Mr Beckett, can you tell us how and when you first became aware of Mr Collins' shortcomings as a teacher?

JB: I'd been aware for some time of rowdy behaviour in some of Jim's classes. Nobody walking past these classes could fail to notice the noise his pupils were making.

JC: Am I allowed to speak?

Chair: You will be given every opportunity to make your case later on, Mr Collins. Go on, Mr Beckett.

JB: I was also aware that Sarah Banks, the head of our science faculty, was in the habit of taking some of Jim's more difficult students out of his classes and supervising them herself. I was concerned that she was spending an excessive amount of time supporting just one member of her team.

PB: When did you first raise your concerns with Mr Collins?

JB: Things came to a head at the beginning of this year. Several parents came to complain that their children weren't making good progress in science and then a group of our more studious Year 11 pupils organised a petition to demand a new teacher to help them through their GCSE exams.

JC: (mutters) Studious, my foot.

PB: (ignoring the interruption) So what did you do?

JB: I talked the problem through with Sarah Banks and then invited Jim to a professional discussion. That was on 10 March...

Mr Beckett then goes through the sequence of events, describing the various methods used to support Jim and the dates on which he received an oral warning, a first written warning and a final written warning. The school produces documents to show that Jim attended a training course in behaviour management and received extensive support from his head of faculty. Evaluation reports from the LEA's science adviser are also produced to show that Jim failed to reach the targets set at each stage of the capability procedure.

After giving his evidence, Mr Beckett is cross-examined by Jim's representative, Brian Searle.

BS: I understand that two of the boys in Jim Collins' Year 9 class were temporarily excluded from school last term and that a number of others were put on report. I put it to you, Mr Beckett, that Jim has had no more difficulty managing in these children than any of the other teachers at the school and yet only he has been singled out for blame.

> Could you explain why my union's member has been victimised in this way?
>
> JB: We do have some difficult children here, but the vast majority are eager to learn and my staff are in the main successful in helping pupils achieve their potential. You mention the Year 9 group that Mr Collins takes for science. If you refer to document 3 in the bundle that you were given before this hearing, you will see that the group's end-of-key-stage results are several percentage points below the national average. Compare these with the results of the parallel group, which are slightly above the national average. There is no difference in the make-up of these two groups. They both contain the same proportion of children receiving free school meals...

After the school's witnesses have given their evidence, the employee or their representative should be given the chance to question each witness in turn. Witnesses other than the headteacher should withdraw after they have finished.

When all of the evidence against the employee has been presented, the employee or their representative will present the case for the 'defence', including any documentary evidence they have to support it. The employee will normally give evidence but is under no compulsion to do so.

The person presenting the school's case will then question witnesses, including the employee if he or she is acting a witness. Again, witnesses other than the employee should withdraw after giving their evidence. Once the employee's case has been presented, he or she should be allowed to sum up the reasons why the complaint should not be upheld.

Either side may ask for an adjournment at any stage in the hearing in order to consider matters. When all of the evidence from both sides has been heard, the employee and their representative must withdraw while the staff dismissal committee makes its decision.

Defence tactics

The aim of those defending an employee at a dismissal hearing is to create doubt in the minds of the panel members that what is happening is fair and reasonable, so the person presenting the school's case needs to anticipate what the trade union official or other representative is likely to say. Very commonly, representatives will claim that the employee has not received adequate support or has not had enough time to improve. It is important, therefore, that any training or other support promised to a struggling member of staff has actually been delivered and that details of these support measures have been systematically recorded.

Another classic defence tactic is to say that other members of staff experience exactly the same problems as the allegedly incompetent teacher. This is where all the statistical evidence that schools are required to collect these days can be very useful. If one teacher's pupils have significantly poorer results than those taught by others, that can provide objective evidence of lack of capability.

Employees facing dismissal will also do all they can to appeal to governors' emotions. It is very difficult to resist such appeals but, if the school has a strong case, it is up to those presenting it to convince governors that they will be abrogating their responsibility to pupils if they allow a clearly incapable teacher to remain in post. Governors should also be on their guard against attempts to manipulate them individually. They should ensure that the outcome of a dismissal hearing is determined behind closed doors while the panel is still properly constituted and that their deliberations are minuted.

The employee's case

Jim and his representative, Brian Searle, use a variety of tactics when they come to present their case:

Chair: I now call on Mr Brian Searle to speak on behalf of Mr Collins.

BS: Our case is quite simple. This school serves a deprived inner-city catchment area. Children who have never known anything but social exclusion are bound to exhibit challenging behaviour in class. None of the documents the school has produced at this hearing prove that Jim is less successful at managing such behaviour than his colleagues.

We have heard from Mr Beckett that Jim is an ineffective teacher, and that his lessons lack pace and variety and fail to motivate more able pupils. I'd now like to call our first witness, Mrs Margaret Harris, who will be able to present a more accurate picture of Jim's ability as a teacher.

Mrs Harris, whose daughter Janice is in Jim's A-level biology class, enters the room.

BS: Mrs Harris, I understand your daughter has just been offered a place to read natural sciences at St John's College, Oxbridge?

MH: Yes, we're very proud of her, and she'd never have got this far if it hadn't been for Mr Collins.

BS: Why is that?

MH: Well, she's always been a very quiet and shy girl, but Mr Collins managed to bring her out of her shell and give her a lot more confidence in herself. It was his idea that she should apply to St John's. She loves his classes, and I just hope the school has the good sense to keep him on. Such a nice, polite young man....

Later Mr Searle calls on Jim to give evidence in his own defence. Towards the end of his testimony, Jim makes the following statement.

JC: All I can say is that Mr Beckett's so-called professional discussion was like a bolt out of the blue. OK, I'd had a few discipline problems in some of my classes, but so had everyone else, and Sarah, my head of faculty, was helping me sort things out. I thought I was doing quite well until the management came along with their bullying tactics. (He gasps for breath and seems unable to continue.)

Chair: Would you like a few minutes to compose yourself, Mr Collins?

JC: No. I just want to remind you that it's my livelihood you've all been discussing so calmly this morning. If I lose my job, I don't see how I'm going support my two kids. One of them's disabled, Mr Beckett. So (turning to the chair of the panel) just ask yourself, Mrs Jones, will you be able to live with yourself if that three-year-old ends up suffering because of the decision you make today?

Despite this strong appeal to their emotions, the governors decide that Jim should be dismissed. He decides to appeal and is suspended on full-pay pending the appeal hearing, which he loses. Never really cut out to be a teacher, Jim is now working as a laboratory technician for a pharmaceutical company.

CHAPTER 5
THE ROLE OF THE GOVERNORS

The new performance management arrangements

The day-to-day running of a school, including the management of staff, should be left to its headteacher. However, education law gives the Governing Bodies of all maintained schools ultimate responsibility for managing teaching and non-teaching staff who are paid out of the school budget.

We strongly recommend that every Governing Body should set up a committee to carry out its responsibilities for personnel matters, although there is no legal obligation to do so.

In relation to staff performance, the Governing Body's main role is to ensure that the school has a written Performance Management policy that meets the requirements of the Department for Education and Employment's performance management framework. This policy should include a commitment to agree, monitor and review objectives with every teacher in the school. Governors also need to make sure that the policy is operating effectively, though they should not become involved in monitoring or evaluating the work of individual teachers.

The performance management framework applies only to teaching staff. Governing Bodies may, however, decide to apply its principles to non-teaching staff as well.

Capability procedures

Where performance reviews, OFSTED inspections, or complaints from parents, pupils or colleagues indicate that a member of staff is not performing to the required standard, governors need to ensure that every stage in the school's capability procedure is followed. The Governing Body should ensure that the capability procedure is reviewed from time to time.

Stages in dealing with lack of capability

1. (The informal stage) Counselling interview or professional discussion, followed, where appropriate, by an oral warning or 'strong advice', preferably from the individual's immediate line manager.

2. First written warning, from either the headteacher or the governors, with a right of appeal to the appeals panel of the Governing Body. In some school procedures, employees are entitled to a second written warning before the final written warning.

4. Final written warning, again from either the headteacher or the governors, with a right of appeal as above.

5. Dismissal by the dismissal committee of the Governing Body, with a right of appeal.

Capability procedures are designed to help employees to improve their performance, rather than to punish, so guidance, support and training, if appropriate, should be given at each stage of the procedure.

Dismissal

By law, the Governing Body must set up a staff dismissal committee made up of at least three members, and a separate appeals committee to hear any appeals against dismissals and final written warnings. Governors involved in making a decision to dismiss a member of staff should not be involved in hearing an appeal against that decision.

The work of the staff dismissal and appeals committees is often highly technical and complex, so Governing Bodies need to make sure they have access to good quality advice about staff dismissal and, indeed, personnel issues generally. Local education authorities are able to provide personnel services but there may be a case for shopping around for quality advice from private sector providers or LEAs other than the school's own authority. Training also has an important role to play in ensuring that members of the governors' dismissal and appeals committees have a sound understanding of the role they might be required to play.

Managing the headteacher's performance

Under the Government's performance management framework, the Governing Body of a school is obliged to review the headteacher's performance with the help of a trained external adviser. The adviser's role is to advise governors on setting performance objectives for the head. Governors may also ask the adviser to manage the process of reviewing the head's performance. Teacher governors should not take part in decisions about how to review the head's performance, nor in the review itself.

The role of the chair of governors in managing a headteacher's performance

Where the review or another source of information suggests that the headteacher's performance is not all it should be, it is up to the chair of the school's Governing Body, as the head's line manager, to deal with the situation. The process is exactly the same as dealing with any other under-performing member of staff.

The first step is to hold a meeting with the head to discuss his or her shortcomings. It is important not to lapse into generalities during this meeting, but to refer to very specific instances of under-performance. The results of regular performance reviews, which should be systematically recorded, will usually inform this discussion.

This discussion should be a two-way process, with the chair of governors giving the headteacher a chance to comment and explain. Possible strategies for improving the head's performance, including in-service training, visits to other schools or mentoring arrangements, should be explored. Finally, the chair of governors will need to tell the head that his or her performance will be monitored over a specified period.

Governors with professional experience of performance management will usually have no trouble in conducting a counselling interview with an under-performing head. For the majority, however, this task is likely to be very difficult. The kind of 'script' that we have already suggested as a way of structuring professional discussions with ineffective staff may therefore be equally useful in relation to ineffective headteachers.

The LEA's role in managing a headteacher's performance

The School Standards and Framework Act gives LEAs a new duty to make a written report to the chair of the Governing Body if they have serious concerns about the headteacher's performance. This duty applies to all categories of maintained school.

According to the *Code of Practice for LEA-School Relations*, the LEA should make such a report only when it has grounds for concluding that the headteacher's performance is having a significantly damaging effect on the school. The LEA is required to send a copy of its report to the headteacher, as well as to the chair of governors. The head should then have an opportunity to make representations to both the chair of governors and the LEA about the report's contents.

The chair of governors must notify the LEA in writing of any action he or she proposes to take in the light of the report. While there is no obligation to accept the report's recommendations, in practice they are likely to trigger formal proceedings against an under-performing head.

Dismissing a headteacher

Until a few years ago, early retirement provided a dignified way out for headteachers who were no longer up to the job. This avenue all but dried up when the government of the day decided that local authorities should contribute to early retirement packages out of their own budgets. Despite new regulations, introduced in April 2000 to enable all teachers, including heads, to take an actuarially reduced pension, it is unlikely that early retirement will ever again become the standard route for dealing with under-performing heads - or teachers, for that matter.

One alternative to early retirement is a legal 'compromise agreement' between the Governing Body and the headteacher. However, if the two sides cannot reach agreement and the situation does not improve, the governors may have no alternative but to consider dismissal. The dismissal process for headteachers is the same as for any other member of staff. The governors' staff dismissal committee considers the case, and there is a right of appeal to a separate committee.

As the head's line manager, the chair of governors will almost certainly have been involved in earlier stages of the capability procedure, and so should not sit on either the dismissal or appeal panel. Nor should the whole Governing Body meet to discuss a vote of no confidence in the head. Such a meeting would immediately prejudice the position of those governors who are on the dismissal and appeals committees, and give a head who has lost an appeal good grounds for bringing a claim for unfair dismissal. The best course of action is to keep the members of these two panels out of any discussion of the head's possible dismissal so that, if they do have to act, their position is not prejudiced.

APPENDIX A
USEFUL ADDRESSES

Advisory Conciliation and Arbitration Service
ACAS Head Office
Brandon House
180 Borough High Street
London SE1 1LW
Telephone 020 7396 5100
(Customer Enquiry Line for London region)
For most enquiries, contact your own regional office
(under Dept of Trade and Industry)

Education Personnel Management
St John's House
Spitfire Close
Ermine Business Park
Huntingdon
Cambridgeshire PE18 6EP
Telephone 01480 431993
Fax 01480 431992
E-mail epm@educ-personnel.co.uk
website: www.epm.co.uk

Institute of Personnel and Development
IPD House
35 Camp Road
London SW19 4UX
Telephone 020 8971 9000 (ask for Enquiry Desk)
Website www.ipd.co.uk (accessible to non-members)

National Association of Governors and Managers (NAGM)
Suite 1, 4th Floor
Western House
Smallbrook Queensway
Birmingham B5 4HQ
Telephone/Fax: 0121 643 5787
E-mail: governorhq@hotmail.com
website: www.nagm.org.uk

National Governors Council
Glebe House
Church Street
Crediton
Devon EX17 2AF
Telephone: 01363 774377
Fax: 01363 776007
E-mail: ngc@ngc.org.uk
website: www.ngc.org.uk

THE EDUCATION PERSONNEL
MANAGEMENT SERIES

THE WELL TEACHER
promoting staff health, beating stress and reducing absence

by Maureen Cooper
ISBN: 1-85539-058-2

Gives clear management startegies for promoting staff health, beating stress and reducing staff absence. Stress is not peculiar to staff in education, but is a common cause of absence. Large amounts of limited schools budgets are spent each year on sick pay and supply cover. This book gives straightforward practical advice on how to deal strategically with health issues through proactively promoting staff health. It includes suggestions for reducing stress levels in schools. It also outlines how to deal with individual cases of staff absence.

MANAGING CHALLENGING PEOPLE
dealing with staff conduct

Maureen Cooper and Bev Curtis
ISBN: 1-85539-057-4

This handbook deals with managing staff whose conduct gives cause for concern. It summarises the employment relationships in schools and those areas of education and employment law relevant to staff discipline. It looks at the difference between conduct and capability, and misconduct and gross misconduct, and describes disciplinary and dimissal procedures relating to teaching and non-teaching staff and headteachers. Throughout the books there are case studies, model procedures and pro-forma letters to help schools with these difficult issues.

Other Network Educational Press Publications

THE SCHOOL EFFECTIVENESS SERIES

Book 1: *Accelerated Learning in the Classroom* by Alistair Smith
ISBN: 1-85539-034-5
- The first book in the UK to apply new knowledge about the brain to classroom practice
- Contains practical methods so teachers can apply accelerated learning theories to their own classrooms
- Aims to increase the pace of learning and deepen understanding
- Includes advice on how to create the ideal environment for learning and how to help learners fulfil their potential
- Full of lively illustrations, diagrams and plans
- Offers practical solutions on improving performance, motivation and understanding
- Contains a checklist of action points for the classroom - 21 ways to improve learning

Book 2: *Effective Learning Activities* by Chris Dickinson
ISBN: 1-85539-035-3
- An essential teaching guide which focuses on practical activities to improve learning
- Aims to improve results through effective learning, which will raise achievement, deepen understanding, promote self-esteem and improve motivation
- Includes activities which are designed to promote differentiation and understanding
- Offers advice on how to maximise the use of available - and limited - resources
- Includes activities suitable for GCSE, National Curriculum, Highers, GSVQ and GNVQ
- From the author of the highly acclaimed *Differentiation: A Practical Handbook of Classroom Strategies*

Book 3: *Effective Heads of Department* by Phil Jones and Nick Sparks
ISBN: 1-85539-036-1
- An ideal support for Heads of Department looking to develop necessary management skills
- Contains a range of practical systems and approaches; each of the eight sections ends with a 'checklist for action'
- Designed to develop practice in line with OFSTED expectations and DfEE thinking by monitoring and improving quality
- Addresses issues such as managing resources, leadership, learning, departmental planning and making assessment valuable
- Includes useful information for Senior Managers in schools who are looking to enhance the effectiveness of their Heads of Department

Book 4: *Lessons are for Learning* by Mike Hughes
ISBN: 1-85539-038-8
- Brings together the theory of learning with the realities of the classroom environment
- Encourages teachers to reflect on their own classroom practice and challenges them to think about why they teach in the way they do
- Develops a clear picture of what constitutes effective classroom practice
- Offers practical suggestions for activities that bridge the gap between recent developments in the theory of learning and the constraints of classroom teaching
- Ideal for stimulating thought and generating discussion
- Written by a practising teacher who has also worked as a teaching advisor, a PGCE co-coordinator and an OFSTED inspector

Book 5: *Effective Learning in Science* by Paul Denley and Keith Bishop
ISBN: 1-85539-039-6
- A book that looks at planning for effective learning within the context of science
- Encourages discussion about the aims and purposes in teaching science and the role of subject knowledge in effective teaching
- Tackles issues such as planning for effective learning, the use of resources and other relevant management issues
- Offers help in development of a departmental plan to revise schemes of work, resources, classroom strategies, in order to make learning and teaching more effective
- Ideal for any science department aiming to increase performance and improve results

Book 6: *Raising Boys' Achievement* by Jon Pickering
ISBN: 1-85539-040-X
- Addresses the causes of boys' under-achievement and offers possible solutions
- Focuses the search for causes and solutions on teachers working in the classroom
- Looks at examples of good practice in schools to help guide the planning and implementation of strategies to raise achievement
- Offers practical, 'real' solutions, along with tried and tested training suggestions
- Ideal as a basis for INSET or as a guide to practical activities for classroom teachers

Book 7: *Effective Provision for Able and Talented Children* by Barry Teare
ISBN: 1-85539-041-8
- Basic theory, necessary procedures and turning theory into practice
- Main methods of identifying the able and talented
- Concerns about achievement and appropriate strategies to raise achievement
- The role of the classroom teacher, monitoring and evaluation techniques
- Practical enrichment activities and appropriate resources

Book 8:   *Effective Careers Education & Guidance* by Andrew Edwards and Anthony
Barnes
ISBN: 1-85539-045-0
- Strategic planning of the careers programme as part of the wider curriculum
- Practical consideration of managing careers education and guidance
- Practical activities for reflection and personal learning, and case studies where
  such activities have been used
- Aspects of guidance and counselling involved in helping students to
  understand their own capabilities and form career plans
- Strategies for reviewing and developing existing practice

Book 9:   *Best behaviour and Best Behaviour FIRST AID* by Peter Relf, Rod Hirst, Jan
Richardson and Georgina Youdell
ISBN: 1-85539-046-9
- Provides support for those who seek starting points for effective behaviour
  management, for individual teachers and for middle and senior managers
- Focuses on practical and useful ideas for individual schools and teachers

Best Behaviour FIRST AID
ISBN: 1-85539-047-7
- Provides strategies to cope with aggression, defiance and disturbance
- Straightforward action points for self-esteem

Book 10:   *The Effective School Governor* by David Marriott
ISBN: 1-85539-042-6
- Straightforward guidance on how to fulfil a governor's role and
  responsibilities
- Develops your personal effectiveness as an individual governor
- Practical support on how to be an effective member of the governing team
- Audio tape for use in car or at home

Book 11:   *Improving Personal Effectiveness for Managers in Schools* by James Johnson
ISBN: 1-85539-049-3
- An invaluable resource for new and experienced teachers in both primary and
  secondary schools
- Contains practical strategies for improving leadership and management skills
- Focuses on self-management skills, managing difficult situations, working
  under pressure, developing confidence, creating a team ethos and
  communicating effectively

Book 12:   *Making Pupil Data Powerful* by Maggie Pringle and Tony Cobb
ISBN: 1-85539-053-3
- Shows teachers in primary, middle and secondary schools how to interpret
  pupils' performance data and how to use it to enhance teaching and learning
- Provides practical advice on analysing performance and learning behaviours,
  measuring progress, predicting future attainment, setting targets and ensuring
  continuity and progression
- Explains how to interpret national initiatives on data-analysis, benchmarking
  and target-setting, and to ensure that these have value in the classroom

Book 13: *Closing the Learning Gap* by Mike Hughes
ISBN: 1-85539-051-5
- Help teachers, departments and schools to close the Learning Gap between what we know about effective learning and what actually goes on in the classroom
- Encourages teachers to reflect on ways in which they teach, and to identify and implement strategies for improving their practice
- Full of practical advice and real, tested strategies for improvement
- Written by a teacher, for teachers, to stimulate thought and interest 'at a glance'

Book 14: *Getting Started: an induction guide for Newly Qualified Teachers*
by Henry Liebling
ISBN: 1-85539-054-X
- An induction guide for newly qualified teachers giving advice on their first year of teaching - how to get to know the school and their new pupils, how to work with their induction tutor and when to ask for help
- Includes masses of practical advice on issues such as getting to grips with the school's documentation, managing pupils' behaviour, time management, classroom management and dealing with tiredness and stress
- Draws on the author's extensive experience as a lecturer and teacher trainer
- Gives NQTs guidance on what to look for when observing experienced colleagues, how to evaluate and develop their own teaching, and to build on their Career Entry Profile to meet the requirements of the induction standards
- Provides an overview of theories in teaching and learning styles, models of teaching, and teaching and learning strategies

OTHER PUBLICATIONS

Imagine that... by Stephen Bowkett
ISBN: 1-85539-043-4
- Hands on, user-friendly manual for stimulating creative thinking, talking and writing in the classroom
- Provides over 100 practical and immediately useable classroom activities and games that can be used in isolation, or in combination, to help meet the requirements and standards of the National Curriculum
- Explores the nature of creative thinking and how this can be effectively driven through an ethos of positive encouragement, mutual support and celebration of success and achievement
- Empowers children to learn how to learn

Helping with Reading by Anne Butterworth and Angela White
ISBN: 1-95539-044-2
- Includes sections on 'Hearing Children Read', 'Word Recognition' and 'Phonics'
- Provides precisely focused, easily implemented follow-up activities for pupils who need extra reinforcement of basic reading skills
- Activities which directly relate to the National Curriculum and 'Literacy Hour' group work. They are clear, practical and easily implemented. Ideas and activities can also be incorporated into Individual Education Plans.

- Aims to address current concerns about reading standards and to provide support in view of the growing use of classroom assistants and parents to help with the teaching of reading

Self Intelligence by Stephen Bowkett
  ISBN: 1-85539-055-8
- Designed to help explore and develop emotional resourcesfulness in yourself and the children you teach
- High self-esteem underpins success in education. More broadly, emotionaly resourcefulness results in improved behaviour and higher standards

Effective Resources for Able and Talented Children by Barry Teare
  ISBN: 1-85539-050-7
- Sequel to *Effective Provisions for Able and Talented Children*
- Provides photocopiable resources for Key Stages 2 and 3
- Arranged into 4 themes: Literacy, Mathematics/Numeracy, Science, Humanities

THE ACCELERATED LEARNING SERIES

Book 1 : *Accelerated Learning in Practice* by Alistair Smith
  ISBN: 1-85539-048-5
- The author's second book which takes Nobel Prize winning brain research into the classroom
- Structured to help readers access and retain the information neccessary to begin to accelerate their own learning and that of the students they teach
- Contains over 100 learning tools and case studies from 36 schools
- Includes 9 principles of learning based on brain research and the author's Seven Stage Accelerated Learning Cycle

Book 2 : *The Alps Approach: Accelerated Leraning in Primary Schools* by Alistair Smith and Nicola Call
  ISBN: 1-85539-056-6
- Takes research collected by Alistair Smith and shows how it can be used to great effect in the primary classroom
- Provides practical and accessible examples of strategies used at a UK primary school where SATs results shot up as a consequence
- Gives readers the opportunity to develop the alps approach for themselves and for children in their care

Book 3 : *Mapwise: Accelerated Learning Through Visible Thinking* by Oliver Caviglioli and Ian Harris
  ISBN: 1-85539-059-0
- This book aims at improving thinking skills through teacher explanation and pupil understanding, and so improves your school's capacity for learning
- Makes teacher planning, teaching and reviewing easier and more effective
- Brilliantly illustrated, it offers the most effective means of addressing the National Curriculum thinking skills requirements by infusing thinking into subject teaching